ESSENTIAL ELEMENTS®

GUITAR ENSEMBLES

EARLY INTERMEDIATE

TOP SONGS 2010–2019

CONTENTS

T0081861

Arrangements by Mark Phillips

ISBN 978-1-5400-5554-5

HAL•LEONARD®

Visit Hal Leonard Online at
www.halleonard.com

Contact us:
Hal Leonard
7777 West Bluemound Road
Milwaukee, WI 53213
Email: info@halleonard.com

In Europe, contact:
Hal Leonard Europe Limited
42 Wigmore Street
Marylebone, London, W1U 2RN
Email: info@halleonardeurope.com

In Australia, contact:
Hal Leonard Australia Pty. Ltd.
4 Lentara Court
Cheltenham, Victoria, 3192 Australia
Email: info@halleonard.com.au

ALL OF ME

Words and Music by John Stephens and Toby Gad

20
E
Bm
A
E
25
Chorus
A
F♯m
D
30
D/E
1.
E
2.
E
34
F♯m
D
A
E
F♯m
To Coda
D.C. al Coda
(take repeat)
Coda
39
D
A
E
A
E

CAN'T FEEL MY FACE

Words and Music by Abel Tesfaye, Max Martin, Savan Kotecha, Anders Svensson and Ali Payami

Chorus
15
Am
G
F
19
Am
G
F
1.
2.
Outro
23
Am
G
27
F
Am
1.
2.

DESPACITO

Words and Music by Luis Fonsi, Erika Ender, Justin Bieber, Jason Boyd, Marty James Garton and Ramon Ayala

Verse

Moderately slow, in 2, with a Latin feel

16
Am
F
20
C
G
24
N.C.
Pre-Chorus
Am
F
4
3
3
28
C
G

32
1.
2.
N.C.
Chorus
Am
36
F
C
40
G
4th time, to Coda
1.
N.C.
2.
N.C.
Verse
Am
44
F
C

48
G
1.
N.C.
2.
N.C.
4
3
Verse
52
Am
F
56
C
G
1.
N.C.
60
2.
N.C.
D.S. al Coda
(take repeat)
Coda
N.C.

GIRL ON FIRE
(Inferno Version)

Words and Music by Alicia Keys, Salaam Remi, Jeff Bhasker, Nicki Minaj and William Squier

15
G♯m
4th time, to Coda
1.
B
2.
D.C. al Coda
(take repeats)
B
Coda
18
B
Bridge
A
B
21
A
B
E
23
C♯m
G♯m
A
E
26
A
B
Outro
E
C♯m

HAVANA

Words and Music by Camila Cabello, Louis Bell, Pharrell Williams, Adam Feeney, Ali Tamposi,
Jeffery Lamar Williams, Brian Lee, Andrew Wotman, Brittany Hazzard and Kaan Gunesberk

Intro

Moderately, with a Latin feel

17
Interlude
Em C B7 Em C B7
21
1. 2.
Em C B7 Em C B7 N.C.
D.S. al Coda 1
(take repeat)
Coda 1
25
Bridge
Em C B7 Em C B7
1. 2.
D.S. al Coda 2
(take repeat)
Coda 2
N.C.

HIGH HOPES

Words and Music by Brendon Urie, Samuel Hollander, William Lobban Bean, Jonas Jeberg, Jacob Sinclair, Jenny Owen Youngs, Ilsey Juber, Lauren Pritchard and Tayla Parx

13
G
F
C
16
Am
1.
Em
2.
N.C.
Bridge
19
C
E+
Am
22
1.
Fm6
2.
Fm6
C
25
E7/B
Am
1.
Fm6
2.
Fm6
D.S. al Fine
(take repeat)

JUST GIVE ME A REASON

Words and Music by Alecia Moore, Jeff Bhasker and Nate Ruess

16
G/B
Am
To Coda 1
Em
To Coda 2
G7sus4
C
D.C. al Coda 1
(take repeats)
Coda 1
20
G7sus4
Bridge
Am
Em
23
F
G
Am
Em
27
F
C/E
Dm
G
N.C.
D.S. al Coda 2
Coda 2
Outro
31
Am
D/F♯
G
C/E
F
C/E
Dm
N.C.
C

NO TEARS LEFT TO CRY

Words and Music by Ariana Grande, Savan Kotecha, Max Martin and Ilya

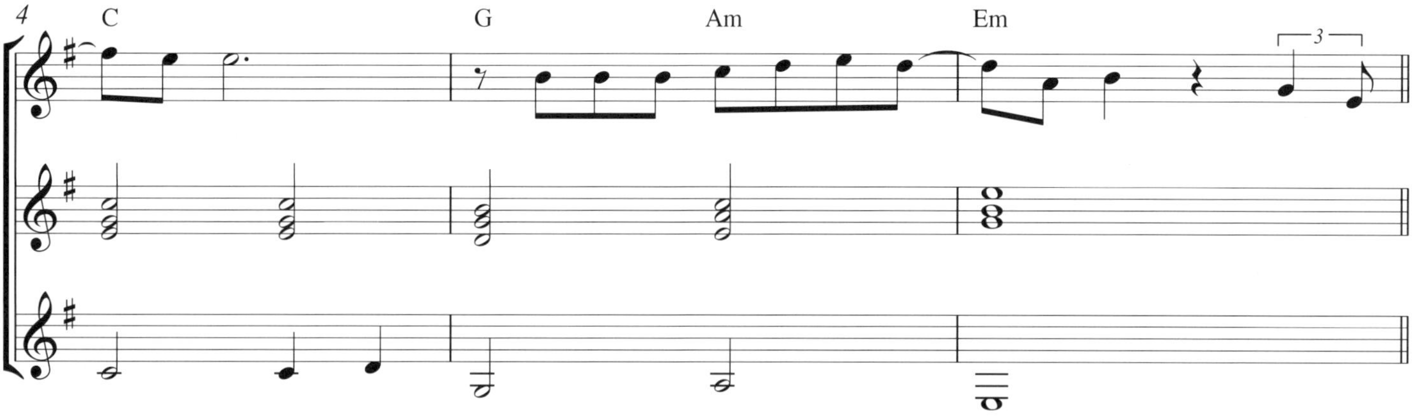

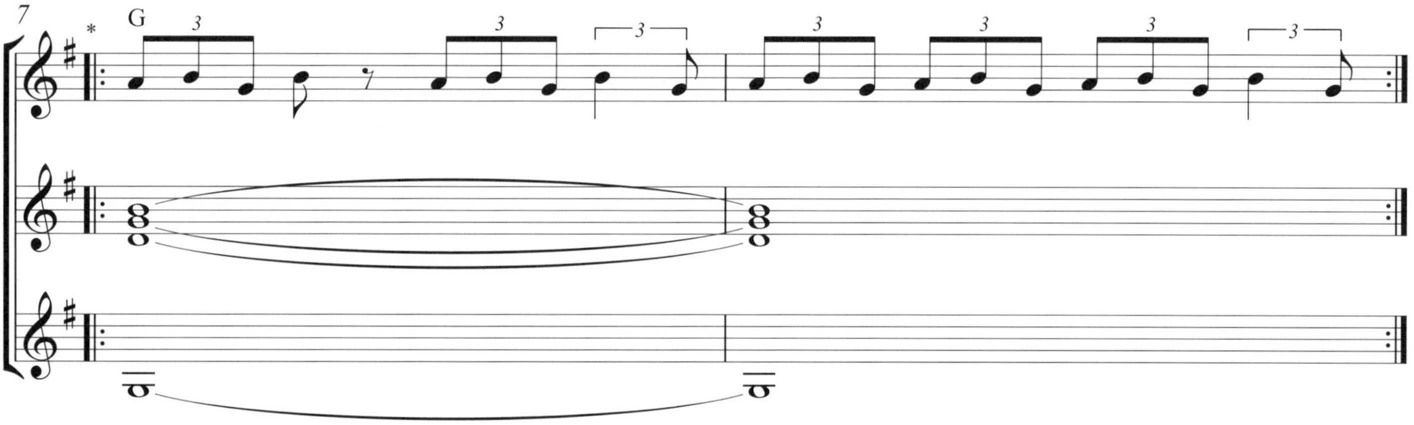

*On *D.C.,* omit repeat (proceed directly to Interlude after 1st time).

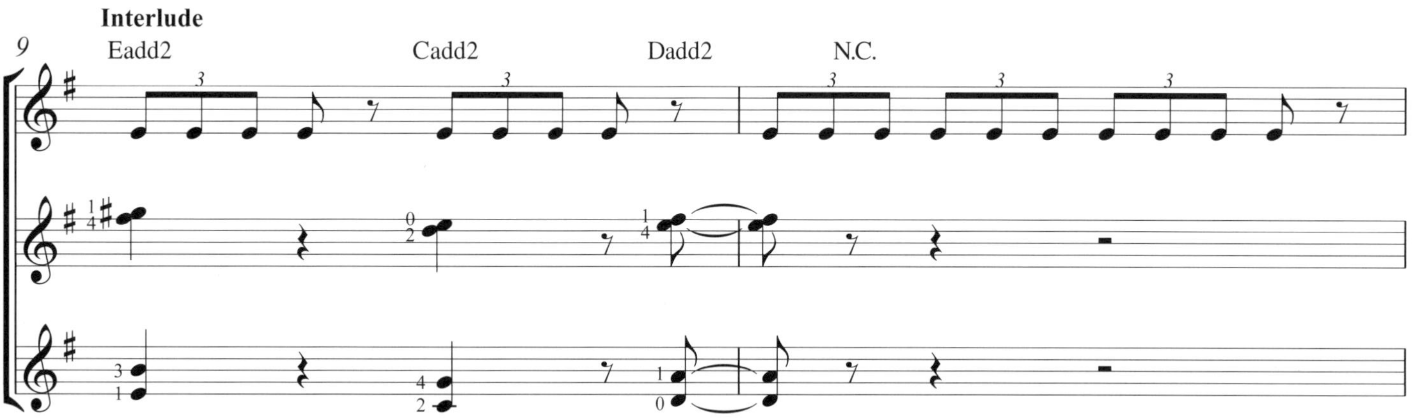

11
Eadd2
Cadd2
Dadd2
N.C.
Fine
Verse
Eadd2
Cadd2
Dadd2
14
N.C.
Eadd2
Cadd2
Dadd2
N.C.
Pre-Chorus
17
Eadd2
Cadd2
Dadd2
N.C.
1.
Eadd2
Cadd2
Dadd2
20
N.C.
2.
Eadd2
Cadd2
Dadd2
N.C.
D.C. al Fine

ONLY GIRL (IN THE WORLD)

Words and Music by Mikkel Eriksen, Tor Erik Hermansen, Crystal Johnson and Sandy Wilhelm

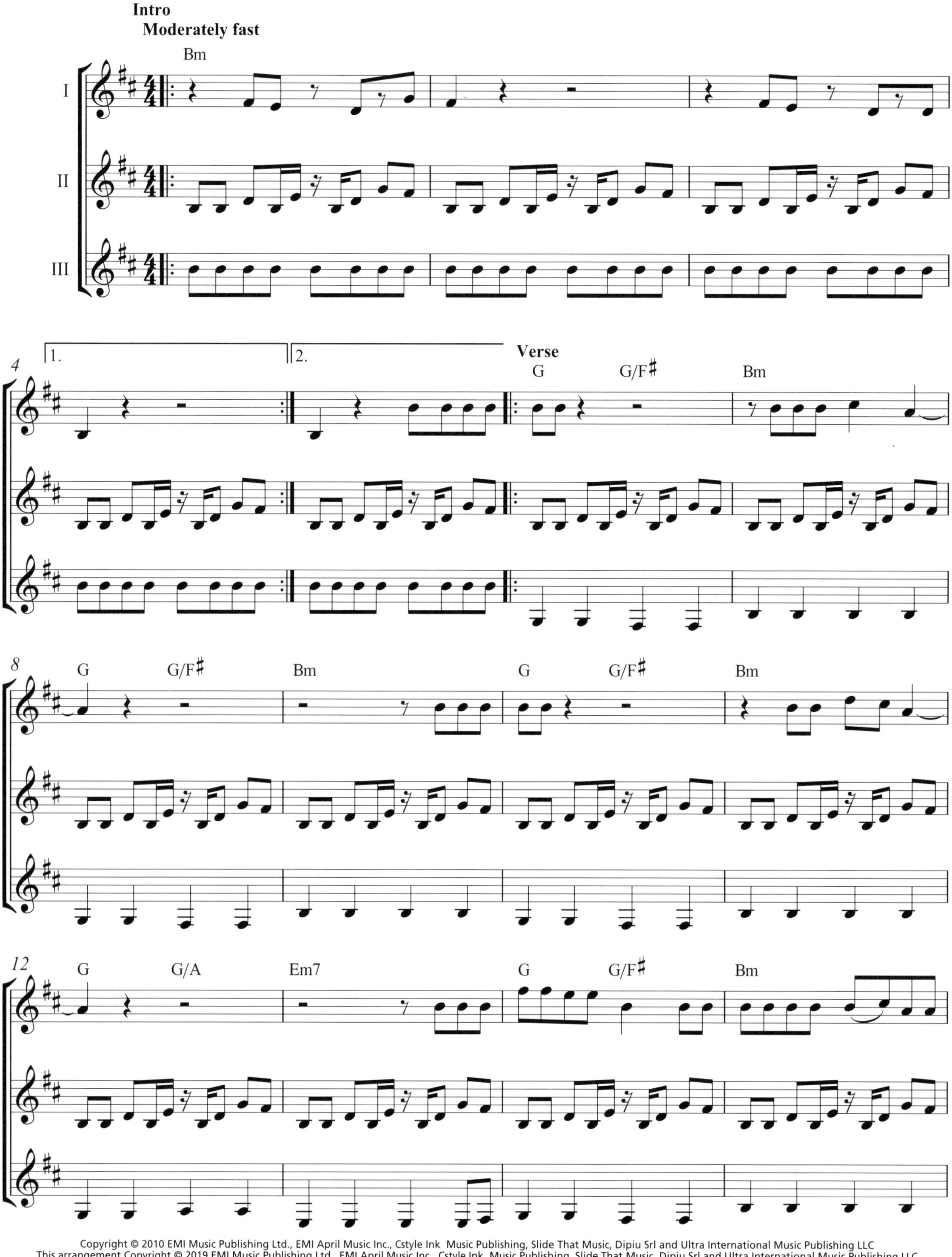

16
G G/F♯ Bm G G/F♯ Bm
20
G G/A Em7
Chorus
C G/C C G/C C D
24
Em D/E Em D/E G C G/C C
1.
G/C C D
28
Am7 G/B C
2.
G/C C D Am7 G/B C

PERFECT

Words and Music by Ed Sheeran

13
G
D
2.
Cadd9
D
N.C.
Chorus
16
Em7
Cadd9
G
D
Em7
Cadd9
19
G
D
Em7
Cadd9
G
D
To Coda
22
Em7
Cadd9
G
D
G
D/F♯
Em7
D
D.S. al Coda
(take repeat)
Coda
25
C
D
N.C.
C
D
G

RISE UP

Words and Music by Cassandra Batie and Jennifer Decilveo

1.
2.
A
E
B
C♯m
To Coda
D.C. al Coda
(take repeats)
Coda
Outro

SHALLOW

from A STAR IS BORN

Words and Music by Stefani Germanotta, Mark Ronson, Andrew Wyatt and Anthony Rossomando

Interlude
17
C♯m7 B/D♯ E C♯m7 B/D♯ E
2.
E B
Chorus
22
F♯m B/D♯ E B
1.
C♯m
26
2.
C♯m
Outro
F♯m F♯m/E B/D♯
1.
E B
30
C♯m
2.
E B C♯m C♯m7

STAY WITH ME

Words and Music by Sam Smith, James Napier, William Edward Phillips, Tom Petty and Jeff Lynne

Gtr. III: Drop D tuning:
(low to high) D-A-D-G-B-E

To Coda
12
E
F♯m7
D
A
C♯7/E♯
15
F♯m7
D
A
1.
2.
Interlude
18
F♯m7
D
A
F♯m7
D
A
21
2nd time, D.S. al Coda
Coda
F♯m
D
A

THAT'S WHAT I LIKE

Words and Music by Bruno Mars, Philip Lawrence, James Fauntleroy, Ray Charles McCullough II, Christopher Brody Brown, Jeremy Reeves, Jonathan Yip and Ray Romulus

13
Am7
Gmaj7
16
Em9
F♯m7
Bm
A
19
B7♯9/F♯
Chorus
Em9
Gmaj7/A
G6/A
23
F♯m7
26
1.
A/B
2.
Bm
A
B7♯9/F♯

EASY GUITAR
WITH NOTES & TAB

This series features simplified arrangements with notes, tab, chord charts, and strum and pick patterns.

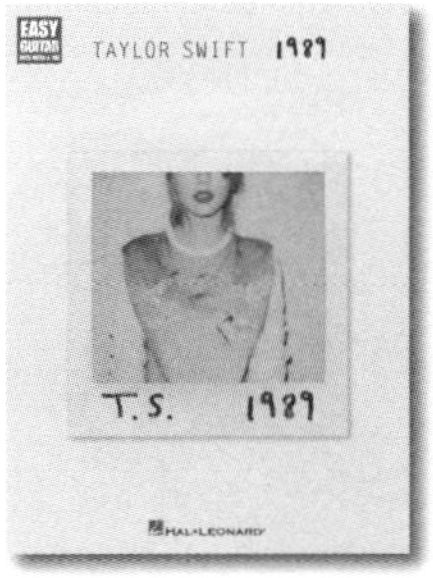

MIXED FOLIOS

00702287 Acoustic $16.99
00702002 Acoustic Rock Hits for Easy Guitar $14.99
00702166 All-Time Best Guitar Collection $19.99
00702232 Best Acoustic Songs for Easy Guitar $14.99
00119835 Best Children's Songs $16.99
00702233 Best Hard Rock Songs $14.99
00703055 The Big Book of Nursery Rhymes & Children's Songs $16.99
00322179 The Big Easy Book of Classic Rock Guitar $24.95
00698978 Big Christmas Collection $17.99
00702394 Bluegrass Songs for Easy Guitar $12.99
00289632 Bohemian Rhapsody $17.99
00703387 Celtic Classics $14.99
00224808 Chart Hits of 2016-2017 .... $14.99
00267383 Chart Hits of 2017-2018 .... $14.99
00702149 Children's Christian Songbook $9.99
00702028 Christmas Classics $8.99
00101779 Christmas Guitar $14.99
00702185 Christmas Hits $10.99
00702141 Classic Rock $8.95
00159642 Classical Melodies $12.99
00253933 Disney/Pixar's Coco $16.99
00702203 CMT's 100 Greatest Country Songs $29.99
00702283 The Contemporary Christian Collection $16.99
00196954 Contemporary Disney $16.99
00702239 Country Classics for Easy Guitar $22.99
00702257 Easy Acoustic Guitar Songs $14.99
00702280 Easy Guitar Tab White Pages $29.99
00702041 Favorite Hymns for Easy Guitar $10.99
00222701 Folk Pop Songs $14.99
00140841 4-Chord Hymns for Guitar $9.99
00702281 4 Chord Rock $10.99
00126894 Frozen $14.99
00702286 Glee $16.99
00699374 Gospel Favorites $16.99
00702160 The Great American Country Songbook $16.99
00702050 Great Classical Themes for Easy Guitar $8.99
00702116 Greatest Hymns for Guitar $10.99
00275088 The Greatest Showman $17.99
00148030 Halloween Guitar Songs $14.99
00702273 Irish Songs $12.99
00192503 Jazz Classics for Easy Guitar $14.99
00702275 Jazz Favorites for Easy Guitar $15.99
00702274 Jazz Standards for Easy Guitar $15.99
00702162 Jumbo Easy Guitar Songbook $19.99
00232285 La La Land $16.99
00702258 Legends of Rock $14.99
00702189 MTV's 100 Greatest Pop Songs $24.95
00702272 1950s Rock $15.99
00702271 1960s Rock $15.99
00702270 1970s Rock $15.99
00702269 1980s Rock $15.99
00702268 1990s Rock $15.99
00109725 Once $14.99
00702187 Selections from O Brother Where Art Thou? $15.99
00702178 100 Songs for Kids $14.99
00702515 Pirates of the Caribbean $14.99
00702125 Praise and Worship for Guitar $10.99
00287930 Songs from *A Star Is Born, The Greatest Showman, La La Land*, and More Movie Musicals $16.99
00702285 Southern Rock Hits $12.99
00156420 Star Wars Music $14.99
00121535 30 Easy Celtic Guitar Solos $15.99
00702220 Today's Country Hits $12.99
00121900 Today's Women of Pop & Rock $14.99
00244654 Top Hits of 2017 .... $14.99
00283786 Top Hits of 2018 .... $14.99
00702294 Top Worship Hits $15.99
00702255 VH1's 100 Greatest Hard Rock Songs $27.99
00702175 VH1's 100 Greatest Songs of Rock and Roll $24.95
00702253 Wicked $12.99

ARTIST COLLECTIONS

00702267 AC/DC for Easy Guitar $15.99
00702598 Adele for Easy Guitar $15.99
00156221 Adele – 25 .... $16.99
00702040 Best of the Allman Brothers $15.99
00702865 J.S. Bach for Easy Guitar $14.99
00702169 Best of The Beach Boys $12.99
00702292 The Beatles — 1 .... $19.99
00125796 Best of Chuck Berry $15.99
00702201 The Essential Black Sabbath $12.95
02501615 Zac Brown Band — The Foundation $16.99
02501621 Zac Brown Band — You Get What You Give $16.99
00702043 Best of Johnny Cash $16.99
00702090 Eric Clapton's Best $12.99
00702086 Eric Clapton — from the Album Unplugged $14.99
00702202 The Essential Eric Clapton $14.99
00702250 blink-182 — Greatest Hits $15.99
00702053 Best of Patsy Cline $15.99
00222697 Very Best of Coldplay – 2nd Edition $14.99
00702229 The Very Best of Creedence Clearwater Revival $15.99
00702145 Best of Jim Croce $15.99
00702278 Crosby, Stills & Nash $12.99
14042809 Bob Dylan $14.99
00702276 Fleetwood Mac — Easy Guitar Collection $14.99
00139462 The Very Best of Grateful Dead $15.99
00702136 Best of Merle Haggard $12.99
00702227 Jimi Hendrix — Smash Hits $16.99
00702288 Best of Hillsong United $12.99
00702236 Best of Antonio Carlos Jobim $14.99
00702245 Elton John — Greatest Hits 1970–2002 .... $17.99
00129855 Jack Johnson $16.99
00702204 Robert Johnson $10.99
00702234 Selections from Toby Keith — 35 Biggest Hits $12.95
00702003 Kiss $12.99
00702216 Lynyrd Skynyrd $15.99
00702182 The Essential Bob Marley $14.94
00146081 Maroon 5 .... $14.99
00121925 Bruno Mars – Unorthodox Jukebox $12.99
00702248 Paul McCartney — All the Best $14.99
00702129 Songs of Sarah McLachlan $12.95
00125484 The Best of MercyMe $12.99
02501316 Metallica — Death Magnetic $19.99
00702209 Steve Miller Band — Young Hearts (Greatest Hits) $12.95
00124167 Jason Mraz $15.99
00702096 Best of Nirvana $15.99
00702211 The Offspring — Greatest Hits $12.95
00138026 One Direction $14.99
00702030 Best of Roy Orbison $15.99
00702144 Best of Ozzy Osbourne $14.99
00702279 Tom Petty $12.99
00102911 Pink Floyd $16.99
00702139 Elvis Country Favorites $15.99
00702293 The Very Best of Prince $15.99
00699415 Best of Queen for Guitar $15.99
00109279 Best of R.E.M. $14.99
00702208 Red Hot Chili Peppers — Greatest Hits $15.99
00198960 The Rolling Stones $16.99
00174793 The Very Best of Santana $14.99
00702196 Best of Bob Seger $12.95
00146046 Ed Sheeran $14.99
00702252 Frank Sinatra — Nothing But the Best $12.99
00702010 Best of Rod Stewart $16.99
00702049 Best of George Strait $14.99
00702259 Taylor Swift for Easy Guitar $15.99
00254499 Taylor Swift – Easy Guitar Anthology $19.99
00702260 Taylor Swift — Fearless $14.99
00139727 Taylor Swift — 1989 .... $17.99
00115960 Taylor Swift — Red $16.99
00253667 Taylor Swift — Reputation $17.99
00702290 Taylor Swift — Speak Now $15.99
00232849 Chris Tomlin Collection – 2nd Edition $14.99
00702226 Chris Tomlin — See the Morning $12.95
00148643 Train $14.99
00702427 U2 — 18 Singles $16.99
00702108 Best of Stevie Ray Vaughan $16.99
00279005 The Who $14.99
00702123 Best of Hank Williams $14.99
00194548 Best of John Williams $14.99
00702111 Stevie Wonder — Guitar Collection $9.95
00702228 Neil Young — Greatest Hits $15.99
00119133 Neil Young — Harvest $14.99
00702188 Essential ZZ Top $14.99

Prices, contents and availability subject to change without notice.

HAL•LEONARD®

Visit Hal Leonard online at **halleonard.com**

0319
306